Aunt Tillie came to Dinner

Aunt Tillie came to Dinner

Written by:
Cynthia Allton

Illustrated by:
Camille Allton

Edited by:
Emily Allton

For Donny,

Who is both an excellent counter
and excellent eater

Aunt Tillie came to dinner one Friday night last fall.
Mom was really glad, since we don't see her much at all.

I took her purse
and hat, and then
I hung them up so
neat.
We chatted just a
bit until Mom
said...

"It's time
to eat!"

We sat up to the table, and soon Auntie cleaned her plate.
She must have been so hungry, for this is what she ate.

Yes she ate:

1 Sandwich

2 pork chops

3 pickles

4 soda pops

5 pancakes

6 boiled eggs

7 brussel sprouts

8 chicken legs

Aunt Tillie was so hungry,
that still she wanted more.

Mom grabbed
her purse
and car keys,

and
headed to
the store...

...Where she bought:

9 bananas

10 tomatoes

11 apples

12 potatoes

13 carrots

14 dinner rolls

15 oranges

16 donut holes

Aunt Tillie ate those groceries, she said she couldn't stop.
But I sure wished she would because I worried she might pop!

NOW she wants...

and...

20
pumpkin pies!

We fed her all that she could hold.
She sat back with a smile.

"I'd like to come again," she said
and then we talked a while.

Aunt Tillie soon asked

"Would you take me
home my dear?
I'd like to take a nap."

And then...

And then she slept for half a year!

The End

www.ingramcontent.com/pod-product-compliance
Lightning Source LLC
Chambersburg PA
CBHW041036120726

48006CB00005B/1212